PUFFIN BO

TUNE I
How TV and Radio Work

How much time do you spend watching television or listening to the radio? Probably quite a lot! But have you ever wondered how your radio and TV sets pick up sound and pictures from thin air?

This original and exciting book not only describes the basic workings of TV and radio, but outlines simple activities which vividly demonstrate them. See how radio waves behave by making waves in a basin of water; use a solar-powered calculator to see how light is turned into electricity in a TV camera; and see how magnetism turns an electric signal into sound. These and other memorable activities, together with lively and revealing illustrations, make this book a perfect introduction to one of today's most common technologies.

Neil Ardley, winner of the 1989 Science Book Prize and *The Times Educational Supplement* Information Book Award, is the author of many books for children on science subjects. Being a keen musician and composer, he has also written on music. He lives in Derbyshire.

Neil Ardley

TUNE IN

How TV and Radio Work

Illustrated by
David Woodroffe

PUFFIN BOOKS

Consultant: Andrew Nahum, Curator of
Aviation, The Science Museum, London

PUFFIN BOOKS

Published by the Penguin Group
Penguin Books Ltd, 27 Wrights Lane, London W8 5TZ, England
Viking Penguin, a division of Penguin Books USA Inc.
375 Hudson Street, New York, New York, 10014, USA
Penguin Books Australia Ltd, Ringwood, Victoria, Australia
Penguin Books Canada Ltd, 2801 John Street, Markham,
Ontario, Canada L3R 1B4
Penguin Books (NZ) Ltd, 182–190 Wairau Road, Auckland 10,
New Zealand

Penguin Books Ltd, Registered Offices: Harmondsworth,
Middlesex, England

First published 1991
10 9 8 7 6 5 4 3 2 1

Text copyright © Neil Ardley, 1991
Illustrations copyright © David Woodroffe, 1991
All rights reserved

The moral right of the author has been asserted

Printed in England by Clays Ltd, St Ives plc
Filmset in Linotron Melior

CONTENTS

Note to readers:

Every effort has been made to ensure that the instructions for the activities in this book are clear and safe. None the less, every care must be taken in the use of such items as scissors and electrical appliances. Care must also be exercised in performing the activities to ensure that injury or damage is not caused. Children must seek adult supervision before attempting these activities.

Remember that the electricity supply to radio and television sets and the electric currents inside sets are strong enough to kill people. NEVER play with electric plugs, power points, and radio and television sets, and NEVER try to take them to pieces.

CHAPTER 1

GOOD VIBRATIONS

AND NOW FOR TODAY'S WEATHER ...

*R*adio and television are marvellous inventions. At the flick of a switch, we can hear voices or music and watch pictures that may come from all over the world. We can even carry a radio or TV set about with us and listen or watch wherever we are. Many people have special radio sets that they can use to talk to other people. The portable telephones that some people carry with them work by radio.

A radio or TV set seems to pluck sounds or pictures out of thin air. In fact, it gets invisible rays that move through the air at immense speed. The rays can also pass through walls to reach the set, just as light rays pass through glass windows to light up a room. In fact, these invisible rays are bombarding us all the time, but we are not aware of them. A radio or TV set can pick up the rays and turn them into sounds or pictures.

SCREECH AND SPEECH

Before you can find out how a radio set makes sounds, you have to know something about sound itself. You can make sounds easily; it's probably the first thing that you did when you were born! Later on, you learned to talk and to sing and maybe also to play music.

Let's see how you make sounds. Take a balloon and blow it up. Then hold the neck between your fingers as shown. Pull to stretch the rubber. A screeching sound comes out as the air leaves the balloon and rushes through the neck. See that the moving air makes the neck vibrate, or move quickly to and fro. Blow up the balloon several times, and alter your pull on the neck. Notice that when you pull lightly, the neck vibrates a lot and the sound is louder. If you pull harder, the neck only vibrates a little and the sound is soft.

It may be hard to believe from the dreadful sound, but you speak in the same way as the screeching balloon! Your own sounds come from the vocal cords inside your neck. The

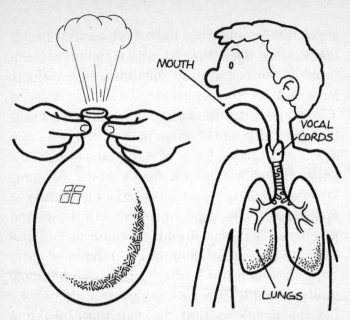

vocal cords are like two elastic bands in your throat. As you speak or sing, air from your lungs passes through a gap between the vocal cords. This is just like air moving through the neck of the balloon. The moving air makes the vocal cords vibrate, and they produce the sound of your voice. Touch your throat lightly as you speak. You can feel the vibration inside.

SOUNDS IN ACTION
When anything vibrates, it makes a sound. Clapping your hands, the rain striking a window, the wind howling, the roar of a passing train, a crash of thunder: all these sounds

come from something that is vibrating. But if we are to hear the sound, it must vibrate quickly – tens, hundreds or thousands of times a second.

In a radio set, the sound comes from a loud-speaker. The earphones in personal stereos are tiny loudspeakers. The loudspeaker has a cone that vibrates quickly at many different speeds. This is why all kinds of sounds – speaking, singing, musical instruments, machines, natural sounds – come out of the loudspeaker when the radio is playing.

If there is a big loudspeaker in your home, you can see it in action. Ask an adult to take off the cover so that you can see the cone

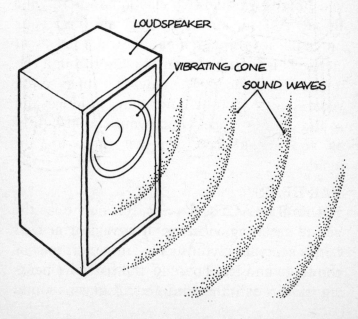

LOUDSPEAKER

VIBRATING CONE

SOUND WAVES

inside. Switch on the radio or play a tape or disc. Turn up the volume so that the sound is loud. You can see the cone vibrating, especially with pop music. Notice how the cone jumps in and out as loud sounds occur in the music. Ask permission to touch the outside edge of the cone lightly: feel how much it is vibrating, but be very careful not to damage the cone.

EAR HEAR

So vibrations cause sounds. But how does the sound reach your ears, and how do you hear it? As something vibrates in and out, it pushes the air to and fro. These to-and-fro movements travel through the air. They make a sound wave. When the sound wave reaches your ears, the moving air enters them. It makes the ear drum inside each ear vibrate too. Tiny bones link the ear drum to the inner ear, which sends signals along a nerve to your brain and you hear the sounds. Strong vibrations give sound waves with strong air movements. These make the ear drums vibrate strongly too, and you hear a loud sound. Weak vibrations give a soft sound.

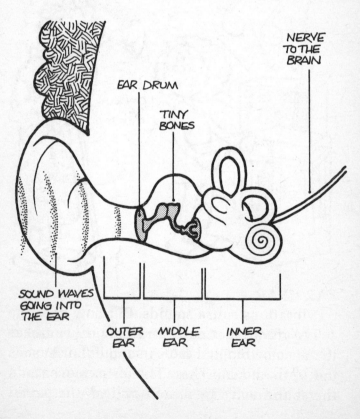

NERVE TO THE BRAIN

EAR DRUM

TINY BONES

SOUND WAVES GOING INTO THE EAR

OUTER EAR   MIDDLE EAR   INNER EAR

You can show this happening. Fix a sheet of paper so that it hangs down in front of the loudspeaker in a radio set. The loudspeaker should be about the size of your hand or larger. Ask permission to turn the radio up loud. See how the paper vibrates as the sounds come out of the loudspeaker. Turn down the volume; see how the paper vibrates less as the sound gets softer.

The vibrating cone in the loudspeaker makes the air move to and fro. A sound wave comes out of the loudspeaker. The air movements in the sound wave push and pull on the paper.

When the sound is loud, the cone moves in and out a lot. It produces air movements that shift the paper strongly. Inside each ear, the ear drum vibrates in the same way as the paper when a sound wave strikes it.

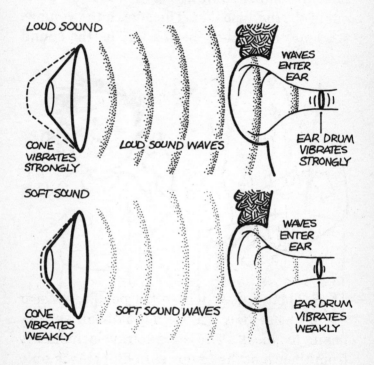

LOUD SOUND

WAVES ENTER EAR

CONE VIBRATES STRONGLY

LOUD SOUND WAVES

EAR DRUM VIBRATES STRONGLY

SOFT SOUND

WAVES ENTER EAR

CONE VIBRATES WEAKLY

SOFT SOUND WAVES

EAR DRUM VIBRATES WEAKLY

CHAPTER 2

SENDING SOUNDS

When we talk with other people, we hear what they are saying as soon as they begin to speak. The sound travels instantly from their mouths to our ears. But this is only because they are close to us. If we could speak to people a long way off, they would not hear us right away and talking to them would be difficult. This is because sound does not in fact travel all that fast; supersonic aircraft can fly faster than sound. Imagine that we could shout a message to someone across the Atlantic Ocean: it would take about eight hours to get a reply!

But the slow speed of sound is not the main problem with sound. Sound waves spread out as they move through the air. This makes the sound get softer as it travels. In fact, sound weakens so much in air that it's hard to hear someone talking on the other side of a large hall. You need to shout in order to talk to someone only a short distance away. To get sounds from one place to another, we need another way of sending them that is fast and does not weaken the sounds.

CARD PHONE

Sound can also travel through solid things. At a railway station or underground station, you can sometimes hear sound coming from the rails before a train arrives. This is the sound of the train wheels. It travels rapidly through the metal rails and gets to the station before the sound of the train arrives through the air. Sounds moving through solid objects travel fast and do not spread out very much.

You can show sound moving in this way by making a simple telephone. Take two carboard tubes. Draw circles on to a piece of card using the ends of the tubes as a guide, and cut out the circles. Make a small hole in each circle of

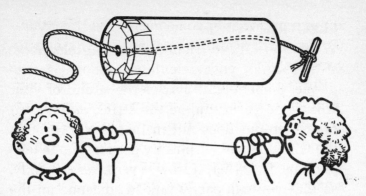

card, and tape the two circles to the ends of the tubes. Take a long length of thin string. Thread the ends through the holes and tie each end around a matchstick, so that the string will not come out of the tubes.

Two people should hold the tubes so that the string is stretched tight. One person speaks softly into one tube while the other person holds the other tube to one ear. The voice can be heard clearly in the telephone. But if the string goes slack, the sound stops.

Speaking into the first tube makes it vibrate with sound, and the sound waves travel along the tight string into the second tube. This tube also vibrates and out comes the sound of the voice. You can see this by plucking the tight string instead of speaking. The whole string vibrates with sound, and you will hear a loud twang in either tube. But a slack string cannot vibrate. This is why the telephone does not work if the string is not tight.

ELECTRIC VOICES

When you talk to friends on a real telephone, a wire links your telephone and their telephone. Somehow, it carries the sound of your voices. However, unlike the string of our card phone, sound does not in fact travel through the wire. Instead, electricity goes from one telephone to the other. It travels very, very quickly, so that you can easily talk to someone on the other side of the world!

Inside the mouthpiece of a telephone is a microphone. As you speak, the microphone changes the sound wave of your voice into an electric signal. The strength of electricity in

the signal changes. It goes up and down at the same rate as the vibrations making the sound wave. This electric signal travels along the wire from one telephone to the other.

At the other end, the electric signal goes to the earpiece. Inside this is a small loudspeaker. The changing electricity in the signal makes the cone of the loudspeaker vibrate. Out comes the sound of your voice. It has been transformed into electricity and back again by the microphone and loudspeaker. Radio uses microphones and loudspeakers in this way too. Let's now see how sound can change into electricity and back again.

SOUNDS WITH MAGNETS

You can show how a loudspeaker changes electricity into the vibrations in sound waves. First take a long steel screw or bolt, and some paper clips. Test the screw or bolt to see if it is magnetic. If it is, it will pick up a paper clip like a magnet. You need a screw or bolt that is *not* magnetic.

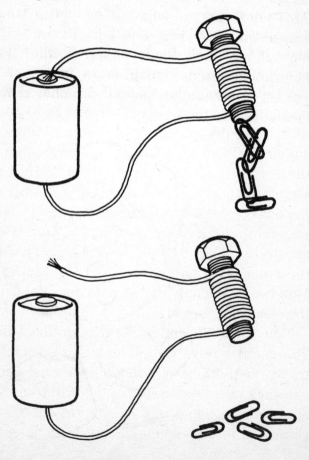

Next take a long length – about a metre – of thin wire with a plastic coating. Wind most of it around the screw or bolt as shown. Always wind the wire in the same direction. Then connect the ends of the wire to a battery; a 9-volt battery should work. Try picking up some paper clips. The screw or bolt has become magnetic. Now remove one end of the wire from the battery. The screw or bolt loses its magnetism, and the paper clips drop off. This device is an electromagnet. It becomes magnetic only when electricity flows through it.

Take a permanent magnet, which is always magnetic. Suspend the electromagnet above one end of the magnet using rubber bands, as shown on page 22. The magnet should pull on the electromagnet so that the rubber bands are stretched tight. Connect one end of the wire to the battery, and the other end to a spoon. Now take another short piece of wire. Connect one end to the other terminal of the battery. Hold the other end of the short wire, and move it. Make sure that moving the wire does not cause the electromagnet to shift.

Now touch the end of the wire on the spoon. The electromagnet should jump slightly as electricity from the battery flows through it and it becomes magnetic. Remove the wire, and the electromagnet jumps back as the electricity stops and it loses its magnetism. Touching the wire on and off several times makes the electromagnet vibrate.

As the magnetism of the electromagnet goes on and off, it alters the pull of the permanent magnet. This is why the electromagnet vibrates. Under the cone of a loudspeaker is an electromagnet and also a permanent

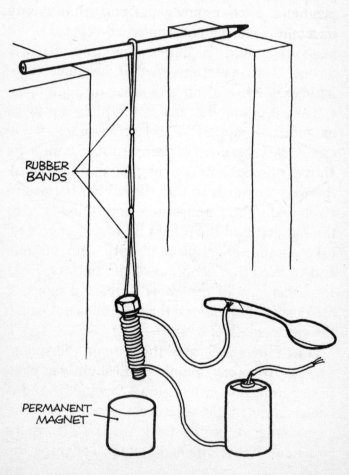

RUBBER
BANDS

PERMANENT
MAGNET

magnet. As the electric signal goes to the electromagnet, the magnetism of the electromagnet changes so that it vibrates. This makes the cone vibrate and it gives out sound.

A microphone works like a loudspeaker in reverse. Sound waves make a part of the microphone vibrate, and this or another part produces a changing electric current. Many microphones use magnetism to do this.

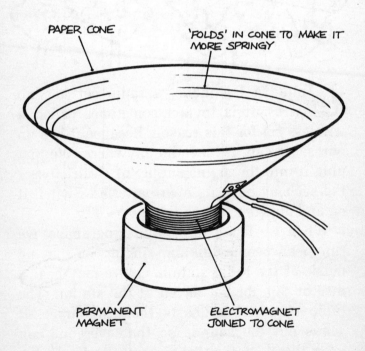

PAPER CONE

'FOLDS' IN CONE TO MAKE IT MORE SPRINGY

PERMANENT MAGNET

ELECTROMAGNET JOINED TO CONE

CHAPTER **3**

WITHOUT WIRES

*U*nlike a telephone, a radio set has no wires. It is in fact sometimes called a wireless set for this reason. Because it has no wires, we can use a radio anywhere. We just plug it into the mains supply of electricity, or the set may have its own batteries. Switch it on and out come the sounds.

When we listen to a radio programme, we can hear people talking, singing or playing music at the radio station. Or we may hear a disc or tape being played at the station. The radio station broadcasts the programme. It sends out the sounds so that everyone can hear them on their radio sets. How do the sounds travel from a radio station to a radio set without wires to carry them?

MAKING WAVES

Invisible rays that we call radio waves carry sounds from a radio station to radio sets. The waves come from the station's transmitter, which is often like a tall metal pole. A radio set has an aerial that picks up the radio waves from the station. The aerial may be inside the set, or it may be a metal rod that projects from the set.

You can see how radio waves travel by making waves with water. Use a bath or sink that has a light above it. Take out any objects in the bath or sink and half fill it with warm water. Now simply dip a finger in and out of

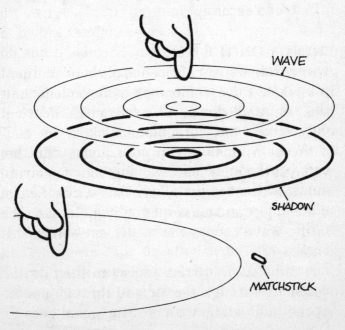

WAVE

SHADOW

MATCHSTICK

the water. A wave spreads out across the water. You can see its shadow on the bottom of the bath or sink. See how the wave spreads out in a circle from your finger. Try dipping your finger several times, both strongly and softly. Notice that the wave always travels at the same speed. Striking the water hard does not make the wave travel faster.

Radio waves travel out from a radio transmitter in circles like the water waves. This is why they can reach radio sets in all directions around the transmitter. Radio waves travel much faster than water waves. In fact, a radio wave can cross the Atlantic Ocean in just one-fiftieth of a second!

ENERGY ON THE MOVE

A wave takes energy from one place to another. In a water wave, the energy is movement that goes up and down. Place a small floating object, like a piece of a matchstick, at one end of the bath or sink. Dip your finger into the water at the other end. Moving your finger up and down makes the wave. This wave travels to the object and makes it go up and down too. So the wave carries the movement across the water.

A radio wave carries energy in the form of electricity through the air and through space. At the radio station, an electric signal goes to

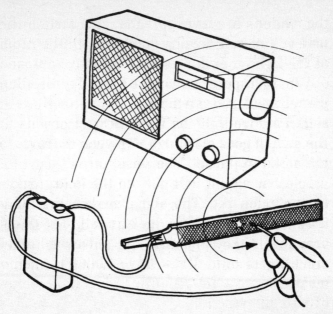

the transmitter and makes it produce radio waves. You can easily show this happening. Take the 9-volt battery and connect two pieces of wire to the terminals. Fasten one end to a steel file as shown. Turn on the radio, and hold the file near the set. Move the other piece of wire along the file. You should see some sparks, especially if the room is dark, and out of the radio should come crackles. Notice that the sparks make the radio crackle. Try changing the wave band control on the radio set, and move the file towards and away from the set. The crackles may get louder or softer. Instead of a battery and file, you can use a light switch that is near a radio set. Make sure your hands are dry first. Turn the switch off, and you should hear a crackle from the radio as the light goes out.

What happens is that the file or light switch makes weak radio waves. This happens as the electricity from the battery or the electricity in the switch goes off and on. The waves travel to the aerial in the set. The aerial turns them into an electric signal that goes to the loudspeaker in the radio set. The signal makes the loudspeaker crackle. The radio waves do not travel very far as they are so weak. This is why the crackle gets softer if the file or switch is further away.

CARRYING SOUNDS

The crackles are just short bursts of noise. The radio wave goes on and off as the sparks occur or the switch is pressed. This gives an on-off electric signal in the aerial, which makes the loudspeaker crackle. How does the radio normally make sounds like voices and music rather than noises?

A person speaks into the microphone at the radio station, or plays a tape or disc player. Out comes an electric signal which changes strength many times a second — at the same rate as the vibrations in the sound waves of the voice or music. When it goes to the transmitter, the electric signal makes the radio wave

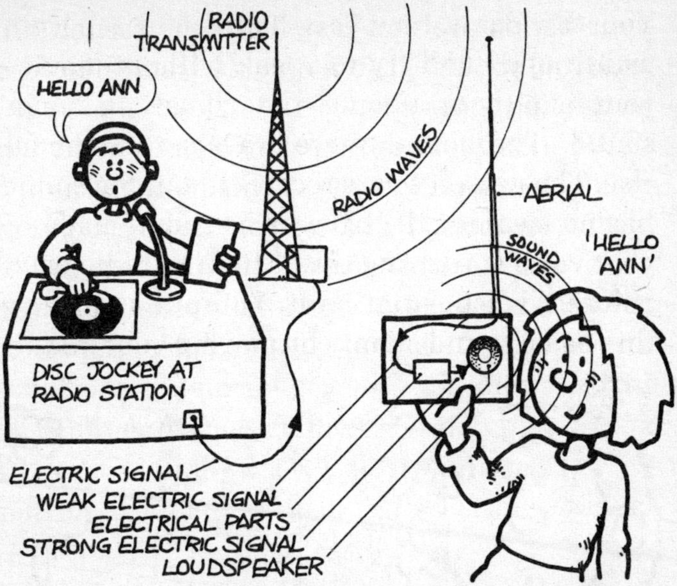
RADIO TRANSMITTER
HELLO ANN
RADIO WAVES
AERIAL
SOUND WAVES
'HELLO ANN'
DISC JOCKEY AT RADIO STATION
ELECTRIC SIGNAL
WEAK ELECTRIC SIGNAL
ELECTRICAL PARTS
STRONG ELECTRIC SIGNAL
LOUDSPEAKER

change strength at the same rate too. The aerial of the radio set receives the radio wave. It then turns the changing radio wave back into the same electric signal as came from the microphone or player. The electric signal in the aerial is very weak, so it goes to electrical parts in the radio set that make the signal stronger. The electric signal finally goes to the loudspeaker in the radio set, and makes the loudspeaker cone vibrate at the same rate as the original sound waves. Out comes the sound of the voice or music.

So the voice or music is 'put' on to the radio wave. It carries a copy of the sound waves from the radio station to your radio set.

You can show how this happens. Keep your mouth open and try to speak without moving your mouth or tongue; out comes an 'aaah' sound. The sound wave travels to someone else. The person's ears receive it, but the sound has no meaning. It is the basic sound made by your vocal cords, and this is like the radio wave before a voice is put on it. You put a voice on this basic sound simply by moving your mouth;

it changes the sound wave so that it carries your voice. In the same kind of way, the radio wave is made to change in order to carry a voice or music. The radio wave is in fact called a carrier wave.

Changing a sound wave or radio wave in this way is called modulation. Radio waves carry sound in two ways: either by amplitude modulation (AM) or frequency modulation (FM). This is why radio broadcasts are either AM or FM.

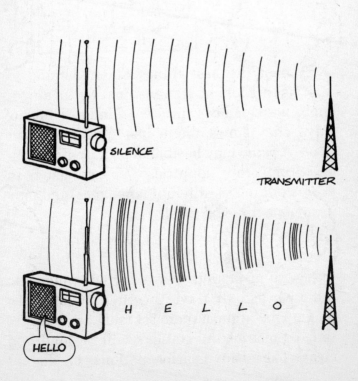

SILENCE

TRANSMITTER

HELLO

H E L L O

CHAPTER **4**

TUNING IN

*O*ne of the best things about a radio is having lots of stations. Just by turning a knob, we can hear different kinds of music, plays, chat shows, phone-ins, talks, news and so on. A radio may be able to pick up programmes from other countries. We can listen to people talking in different languages, and may hear some unusual music.

RADIO RANGE

Every radio station has a certain range. Its radio waves only travel a certain distance. To pick up a station, a radio set must be inside its range. Some of the stations will be loud and clear. These are nearby stations, or distant stations with a long range. Other stations are quiet because the set is at the end of their range. You have to turn up the volume to hear them.

The aerial of the set picks up the radio waves from all the different stations within range. Try getting different stations on your radio. This is called tuning. You turn the tuning control to tune the radio to different stations. When you can hear one clearly, move the aerial and remove your hand, or turn the whole radio set if the aerial is inside the set. The sound may fade away or may crackle or hiss as you do this; if it doesn't, try another station, especially an FM station. The sound changes because of the direction of the radio station. The radio waves coming from the station do not strike the aerial full on. Turning the aerial or set lets the radio waves strike it properly.

TURNING THE AERIAL TO GET GOOD RECEPTION

SHORT OR LONG, QUICK OR SLOW

A radio set can get lots of different stations or programmes because each one has a different kind of radio wave. The aerial turns all the waves into many electric signals. Tuning the radio chooses just one signal and rejects all the others. This signal goes to the loudspeaker in the radio set, and out comes the programme or station that you choose.

What is different about all these radio waves that come through the air to your set? You can

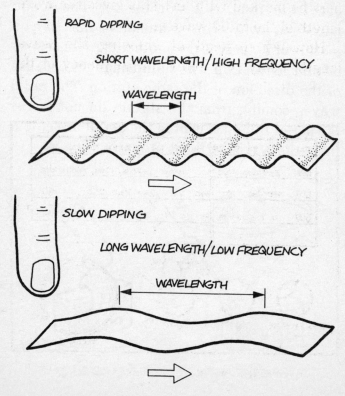

RAPID DIPPING

SHORT WAVELENGTH / HIGH FREQUENCY

WAVELENGTH

SLOW DIPPING

LONG WAVELENGTH / LOW FREQUENCY

WAVELENGTH

show the difference by returning to the water in the bath or sink. Dip your finger into the water quickly several times. See that the waves are close together. Dip your finger slowly and the waves are farther apart. The distance between the waves is called the wavelength.

All the radio waves that come to your set have different wavelengths. When you tune the set, you select a station or programme with a certain wavelength. You turn the tuning control to a certain number on the dial. This number may be marked with 'm'. This gives the wavelength of the radio wave in metres.

However, instead of showing the wavelength, many sets show the frequency of the

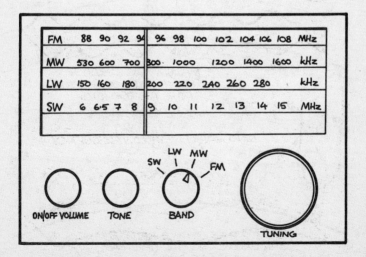

radio waves. Each station or programme has its own particular frequency as well as a wavelength. The frequency is the rate at which the radio waves arrive at your set. The frequency is marked with MHz or kHz: MHz means millions of waves arrive each second and kHz means thousands of waves arrive every second. If the wavelength of the radio wave is shorter, its frequency is quicker.

FAVE WAVES
To get lots of stations, you need a radio set with several wave bands. Most radio sets have

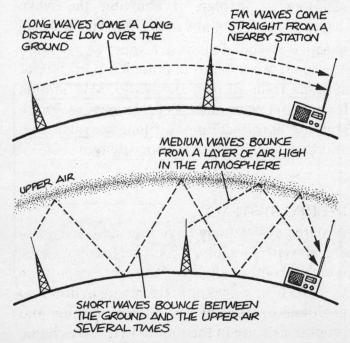

LONG WAVES COME A LONG DISTANCE LOW OVER THE GROUND

FM WAVES COME STRAIGHT FROM A NEARBY STATION

MEDIUM WAVES BOUNCE FROM A LAYER OF AIR HIGH IN THE ATMOSPHERE

UPPER AIR

SHORT WAVES BOUNCE BETWEEN THE GROUND AND THE UPPER AIR SEVERAL TIMES

up to four wave bands. These are marked FM (or VHF), SW, MW and LW. You choose a wave band with the wave band control. Then you turn the tuning control to get all the different stations or programmes in the wave band. Choosing another wave band gets more stations.

FM stands for frequency modulation. This is a way of sending sounds by radio that gives the best sound quality. However, the range is short so FM stations are nearby. FM stations are in the VHF (very high frequency) band. As their frequency is very high, the wavelengths are very short.

SW stands for short wave, and the stations in this wave band all have a short wavelength. The short wave band is crowded with lots of stations from all over the world. MW stands for medium wave and LW for long wave. These stations have medium and long wavelengths, and they may be close or fairly distant.

STEREO SYSTEMS

A stereo system may have tape and disc players as well as a radio. It has two loudspeakers, which produce slightly different sounds so that you hear voices or instruments in different positions in front of you. Stereo stations and programmes are in the FM or VHF wave band.

A stereo system may also have a graphic equalizer. As you operate the controls, the quality of the sound changes. You can hear this best with a voice rather than music. Every sound is in fact a mixture of low, medium and high parts. The controls make these parts of the sound louder or softer. You should set the controls to get the best sound. The controls are marked in Hz or kHz. This is because low, medium and high sound waves have different frequencies. Sound waves have much slower frequencies than radio waves.

CHAPTER 5

PICTURES FROM THE AIR

*T*elevision is a window on the world. Watching a TV set is like looking through a window that can suddenly move anywhere in the world. Of course, television would not be much good without sound too. The sound comes by radio, and a TV set has a loudspeaker that works in the same way as a radio set. But how does a TV set pluck a moving picture from thin air? Let's first look at the picture and see how it moves.

FREEZING THE FRAME

Suppose that everything, except for you, suddenly went very slow. People would move about as if they were half asleep; a ball would take a long time to fly through the air. And if you were watching television, you would expect that the picture would move slowly too. In fact, it would not move at all! Instead, you would see a lot of still pictures. One still picture after another would flash up on the screen. You would see that a smooth movement like a waving arm had become a set of still pictures showing the arm 'frozen' in different positions.

Of course, it's impossible to slow everything down to see this. However, you can show that it happens if you have a video recorder. Ask an adult to operate the video recorder for you. First, record part of a TV programme with some fast action, like someone diving into water. Then rewind the tape and start to play it back. Press the pause button. The action stops and you see a still picture of the person on the screen: the diver could be hanging in

mid-air! The still picture is called a frame, and it is just like a picture taken with a camera. No matter where you stop the tape, you will always see a still picture of the action taking place on the screen. This is because the TV programme was made of still pictures, and the video records these pictures one after the other. The video recorder may have a button that will move through the frames so that you can see one after the other.

So a TV set does not in fact pluck a moving picture from the air. Instead, it gets lots of still pictures — 25 still pictures every second. But because it shows these pictures so quickly, the still pictures merge together in our eyes. We do not see one still picture changing into the next. Instead, we see a smooth movement. Let's see how our eyes trick us in this way.

COMIC STRIP

Photocopy page 42 of this book. It contains 16 strips each with a picture. Carefully cut the copy up into the strips. Then take a notebook or old exercise book. Paste each strip along the edge of a right-hand page in the book. Start with strip 1 on the first right-hand page, then paste strip 2 to the second right-hand page, and so on as shown. Make sure to paste the top of each strip at the top of each page.

When you have finished, hold the book in

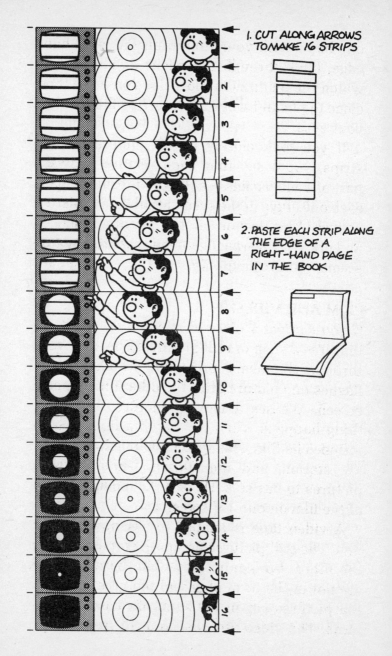

1. CUT ALONG ARROWS TO MAKE 16 STRIPS

2. PASTE EACH STRIP ALONG THE EDGE OF A RIGHT-HAND PAGE IN THE BOOK

one hand with your thumb on the right-hand edge. Flick through the pages as shown and watch the pictures in the strip. You'll see them come to life and move as the strips flash before your eyes.

If you look closely at the pictures in the strips, you'll see that each picture shows a part of a movement. As the pictures flash past, each one stays in the eyes until the next picture arrives. You do not see the pictures flash on and off. They merge together so that the picture seems to move smoothly.

FILM AND VIDEO

If you can get a piece of movie film, you'll see that it is a strip of still pictures. The strip goes through a cinema projector, which quickly flashes one picture after the other on a cinema screen. We see a moving picture. The same thing happens when we watch a film on television. The film goes through a machine at the TV station, and the station sends the still pictures to our sets. We see the moving action of the film on our TV screens.

A video tape is similar to a strip of movie film. The still pictures are on the tape one after the other. We cannot see them because they are not in the form of actual pictures. Instead, the pictures are in the form of magnetic patterns. The video recorder and TV set change the magnetic patterns on the tape into the moving picture we see on the screen.

In fact, many of the programmes that come from a TV station are video recordings. Only programmes that are 'live' are actually happening as we watch them. The others are films or are programmes that have been recorded on video tapes. A video recorder at the TV station plays the tape, and the station sends the pictures on the tape to our TV sets.

CHAPTER 6

IN THE CAMERA

*T*he studio at a television station is a very exciting place. It's often a huge room, packed with bright lights. The people we see in the programme are on the studio set, which has furniture or scenery like a small stage. In front of them are several TV cameras. The cameras move about to get different views of the people. Television presenters often talk to the camera as if they were talking just to us. However, they are usually reading words that come up on a screen placed beside the camera!

Each TV camera makes the pictures that come through the air to our TV sets. The director of the programme chooses which camera is on at any time. Instead of using a studio, the cameras may be outside – at a sports event for example. Often a video recorder is connected to the cameras. It stores the pictures on tape so that they can be shown later.

CARDBOARD CAMERA

A TV camera is very like the kind of camera that takes photographs. It has a lens that forms an image inside the camera. You can see how this happens by making a simple camera.

Take a box of stout cardboard and a cardboard tube. Cut a hole for the tube in one side of the box; the tube should fit tightly but be

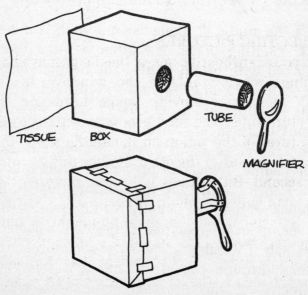

TISSUE   BOX   TUBE   MAGNIFIER

able to move in and out. Then cut off the opposite side of the box and tape a tissue over it. Take care with scissors.

Next take a plastic magnifier and tape it to the end of the tube. Hold the cardboard camera up to face a window, and you will see an image of the window on the tissue paper. Move the magnifier in or out until the image is sharp. If you have a magnifying glass, use this instead of a plastic magnifier as it works better. You can hold it over the end of the tube.

The magnifier is the lens of the TV camera. The tissue is the surface of a picture tube in the TV camera. You'll see that the image is upside-down. But this does not matter as the TV set will turn it the right way up.

ELECTRIC PICTURES

In your cardboard camera, the image may show things moving outside the window. In the TV camera, a moving image forms on the picture tube. The tube produces separate still pictures of the action on the studio set or in a match, one after the other. It does this 25 times a second. But it does not make pictures that we can hold like photographs.

Remember how a microphone in a radio station changes the sound of a voice or music into electricity? A TV camera does the same for the light in the image on the picture tube. It

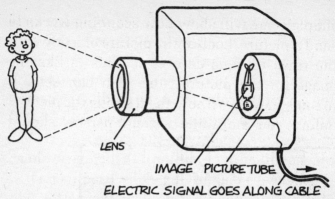

LENS

IMAGE PICTURE TUBE

ELECTRIC SIGNAL GOES ALONG CABLE

turns all the light into an electric signal. This takes 1/25 second. Out of the camera comes the electric signal. The TV station broadcasts this signal by radio. The radio wave has the pattern of light in the picture 'put' on it in the same way as a radio wave may also carry sound.

The aerial of a TV set picks up the radio waves and produces the electric signal again. The set turns the signal back into a still picture that we see on the screen. Then the camera starts again and sends the next picture. As we watch, 25 pictures arrive every second and we see the moving image formed by the camera lens.

TV GAME

In fact, the TV camera does not send a whole image at once. It breaks the picture into little pieces, and the TV set puts the pieces back together again. This is called scanning. A simple game will show how scanning works to send a picture. Look at the picture of a dog with the rows of squares over it. This is like the image on the picture tube. You can send it to someone else without them seeing the picture. Before you start, the second person should

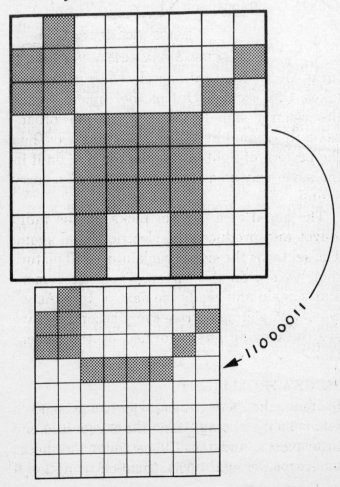

mark the same rows of squares on a piece of blank paper. This paper will be the screen of the set, and can be bigger or smaller.

The first person starts with the square in the top left-hand corner. He or she says a number that gives the amount of light in the square. Use 0 for black, 1 for white. The second person fills in the same square with a pencil, making it black or white as the number said. Continue with the squares along the top row. Then do the second row down and continue until the picture is finished. The second person will have made a copy of the picture. Draw your own pictures and send them to each other.

You send the pictures to each other in the same way as happens in television. The picture will not be very good, and you may have to look at it from a distance to see it. But this is only because you have not used many squares or a wide scale of numbers for the light. If you were to use several thousand squares with a much wider scale, then you would get a good picture. A TV set does this 25 times a second!

POWER FROM LIGHT

Scanning happens very quickly in television. The camera tube splits up the image into 625 thin strips called lines. It looks along each line and turns the brightness of each little part of it into electricity. This gives an electric signal that changes in strength. If the part is bright, the signal is strong; when it is dark, the signal is weak. As it scans the image, the camera turns the changing pattern of light and dark in the image into a changing electric signal.

If you have a solar-powered calculator, you can see how the camera tube turns light into electricity. The calculator gets power from its solar cells, which turn light into electricity. Cover up the solar cells with your hand or some cardboard. The display that shows the numbers will fade. This is because the calculator is not getting any electricity. Take the calculator to a window or near a light bulb. Uncover the cells. The display quickly comes back. This is because the cells are turning the

bright light into strong electricity. Cover up the cells again. Then uncover them in a dim part of the room, or shade them from the light with your hand. The display now takes some time to come back. This is because the dim light does not give so much electricity.

In the tube of a TV camera, the image falls on materials that are sensitive to light. They change light into electricity like the solar cells in a calculator.

CHAPTER 7

OVER AND UNDER THE GROUND

*J*ust like a radio set, we can switch on a TV set and get several different stations or programmes. These are often called television channels. Radio waves broadcast by the stations from high masts carry the pictures. Each channel uses a radio wave with its own wavelength. When we press the channel button, the set tunes into a particular wavelength and we see the channel we want.

There are not as many TV channels as there are stations on the radio. We cannot tune into TV programmes from distant countries. This is because the radio waves from TV stations travel in a straight path and do not travel around the Earth. So the stations have a short range. In the countryside, there are many small TV masts that broadcast channels to towns and villages around. Signals come through wires to these masts.

A television set needs an aerial to pick up the radio waves from the nearest mast. Unless the mast is close to a home, the aerial may have to be fixed outside. This is because the radio waves from a distant mast are not strong enough to pass through the wall of the house. The aerial must be in the right position. Then it will produce a strong electric signal that will give a good picture on the set. Moving the aerial can cause the signal to weaken so that the picture breaks up or disappears.

PICTURES FROM SPACE

Many TV sets can get satellite channels. These pictures still come by radio waves. But a mast does not send them out. Instead, the TV station sends the radio waves up to a satellite out in space, and the satellite sends them back down. We cannot see the satellite because it is so far away. It travels around the Earth at the same speed as the Earth turns. The satellite therefore stays in the same place above the Earth all the time.

The radio waves from the satellite spread out to cover a wide area – even a whole country. But because the satellite is so far away, the radio waves are very weak. The set needs a special aerial to pick them up. This aerial may have a big dish. It has to point at the satellite. The dish strengthens the radio waves. It gathers the waves so that they collect at a central metal rod, which is the aerial.

You can show how a dish aerial works with a plastic ruler and some marbles. One person bends the ruler into a shallow curve, like the dish, and holds it up on one side on a bare table top. A second person rolls the marbles

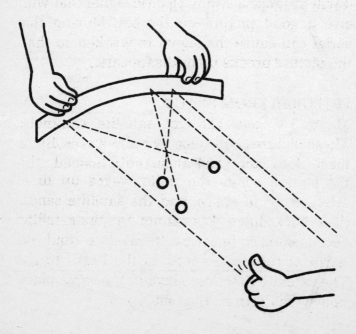

along the table top into the curve. See how the marbles bounce off the ruler. If the curve is the right shape, the marbles will always bounce to a point in front of the centre of the curve. This is called the focus.

In a satellite dish, the aerial is at the focus. The radio waves are like the marbles. They strike the dish and then bounce off to meet at the aerial. The aerial gets lots of waves and produces a strong signal for the TV set. There is another type of satellite aerial which looks like a flat square plate. Inside it are many very small dish aerials, each one of which gives a weak signal. The small dishes are linked together to increase the signal.

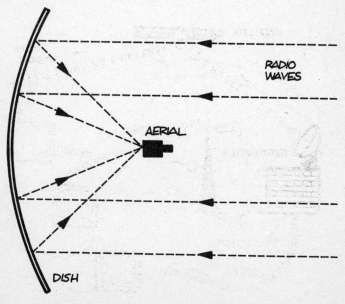

LAND LINKS

Not all TV channels come by radio waves. Cable television does not use radio at all. Instead, the cable station uses a cable containing wires. The station sends out the electric signals from the cameras or video recorders. The signals travel along a cable under the ground to a home and go straight to the TV set. There is no aerial.

Cable television gives very good pictures because the signal is strong. The station sends out several channels along the cable. These may include broadcast channels as well as extra channels, for example, a channel that shows only films.

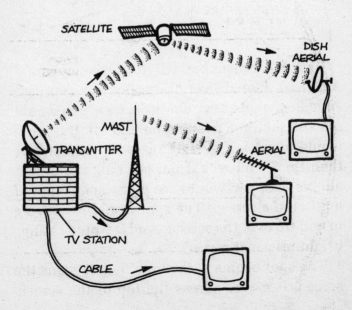

CHAPTER 8

SCANNING THE SCREEN

I CAN SEE SPOTS BEFORE MY EYES!

Do you remember what television would look like if everything (except yourself) suddenly went slow? On the screen, you would see still pictures flashing on and off. But what would you see if everything went even slower than this? You would not see still pictures at all. Instead, you would see just a small spot of light on the screen. The spot would be moving to and fro over the screen. And it would change brightness as it moved.

The spot begins at the top. Then it scans the screen. It moves across the top of the screen, then goes back and down slightly before moving across again. The spot covers the whole screen before starting at the top again.

We cannot make out this spot of light when we watch television because it moves very, very fast. It covers the whole screen in just 1/25 of a second. Our eyes do in fact see the spot, and its light stays in the eye for a short time. In this time, the spot covers the whole screen. As its brightness changes, the spot builds up a still picture in the eye. It rebuilds the image that is split up into pieces inside the TV camera.

AN IMAGE IN THE AIR

You can show how a TV picture builds in the eye if you have a slide projector. This activity works best when it is dark, especially if you can point the projector out of an open door or window. Ask an adult to switch on the projector and put a slide in it. Using a piece of blank paper, focus the picture a short distance in front of the projector. When you take the paper away, the picture may appear on the wall of the room but should be very blurred.

Now take a rod or stick. Switch off the light. Stand by the place where the picture was in focus. With care, quickly move the rod through the beam of light from the projector. The picture will briefly appear in mid-air! Move

the rod quickly up and down to see the picture for longer. If you do not have a rod or stick, your arm might work instead.

What happens is that the projector forms an image of a thin strip of the slide on the rod. As the rod moves down, the image on it changes from a strip of the picture at the top down to a strip at the bottom. But each strip briefly stays in the eye after the rod moves on. All the thin strips build up a whole picture.

LIGHTING-UP TIME

A TV set builds up a picture in the same way. Instead of strips, the picture builds up with 625 lines. These are the same as the lines in the camera tube. The set keeps in step with the camera so that they both scan exactly together. As the camera scans the top line of the image on the tube, a glowing spot speeds across the top of the screen. It changes brightness to trace out the top line of the picture. Then the rest of the lines follow. So a bright or dark part of the image formed by the camera lens on the camera tube produces a bright or dark spot in the same place on the screen. Every second, 25 still pictures are scanned in this way, and our eyes merge them into a moving picture.

How does the screen of the TV set light up? The screen is the front of a special glass picture tube. At the back of this tube is an electron gun. It's not a weapon of any kind. The gun fires a beam of electrons at the screen. Electrons are tiny particles of electricity. As they strike the inside of the screen, the electrons make a special coating on the screen glow with light.

The TV set produces an electric signal that comes either from its aerial or along a cable. This is the same as the signal that left the camera or video recorder at the TV station.

The signal goes to the electron gun and makes it send out the electron beam, which scans across the screen. The electric signal changes strength depending on the brightness of each part of the picture. It makes different amounts of electrons strike the screen as the beam moves. A glowing spot lights up on the screen and moves over it. The spot changes brightness as the strength of the signal changes so that the picture builds up.

What makes the electron beam move? In the tube are coils of wire that work like electromagnets. They become magnetic and push or

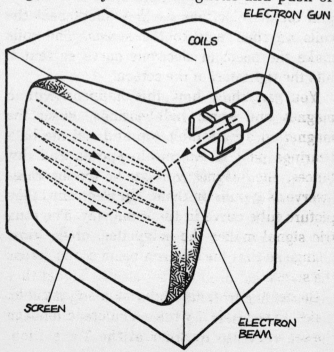

ELECTRON GUN

COILS

SCREEN

ELECTRON BEAM

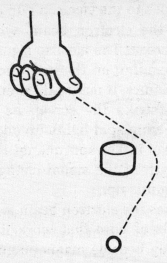

pull on the electrons as they shoot past the coils on their way to the screen. The coils make the beam of electrons curve so that it hits the right part of the screen.

You can show how this happens with a magnet and some ball-bearings. Place the magnet on a bare table top and roll the ball-bearings past it. At certain speeds and distances, the magnet will make the bearings swerve as it pulls on them. The electrons in the picture tube curve in the same way. The electric signal makes the magnetism of the coils change so that the electron beam scans across the screen.

Do **not** try to open a television set and look inside to see how it works. You could damage the set and badly hurt yourself.

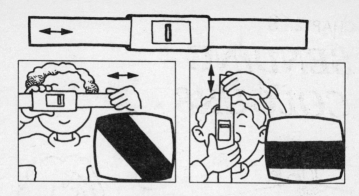

OUT OF THE PICTURE

Although you cannot actually see the spot moving in a TV picture, you can show that scanning does happen. Cut a long strip of paper and make a narrow slot in it as shown. Next fix a short length of paper around the strip. First cut a rectangular hole in the paper so that the slot can slide past the hole. Take care with scissors.

Place the paper strip in front of one eye. Close the other eye, and look through the hole and slot at a TV screen. Move the slot to and fro quickly. The picture should go strange. You should see black stripes on it.

This happens because you see the screen for only a very short time as the slot passes the eye. It's like seeing a very quick snapshot of the screen. The glowing spot does not have time to build the whole picture. So you see only part of the picture. The rest of the screen is blank and looks black.

CHAPTER 9

SENDING COLOURS

You may have noticed that one important thing has been missing from our television picture. It's had no colour, and was only in black and white. The camera sent only the brightness of each part of the scene to the TV set. It did not send the colour of each part.

The first television sets showed black-and-white pictures. Small sets and cheaper sets still work in black-and-white. Shops and stores use black-and-white sets for checking that people do not steal. Cameras watch the customers, and send electric signals along wires to a TV set. This use of television is called closed-circuit television.

Television channels are now in colour. You need a colour set to get a colour picture. Black-and-white sets can pick up colour programmes, but they show them only in black and white.

SEEING RED ... GREEN AND BLUE

A colour TV set can show us all the colours that our eyes can see. The screen lights up in hundreds of different shades. Or so it seems. In fact, we are seeing only three colours and not hundreds. These three colours are red, green and blue. We may see yellows, purples, pinks, browns, oranges ... and white too. But they are all mixtures of red, green and blue!

You can show this with a magnifier or magnifying glass. Switch on a colour set, and look closely at the screen with the magnifier. The picture is not like an ordinary picture at all. It's made of lots of little dots or stripes. These light up in red, green and blue, and each one may be bright or dark. When you look at the screen from normal viewing distance, the tiny dots and stripes merge together in the eye to form a picture.

The eye mixes the three colours to give all the different shades of colour. See how red and green give yellow, for example. And red, green and blue together give white. You can see this by turning the colour control so that the picture goes black and white. Black occurs where none of the dots or stripes light up.

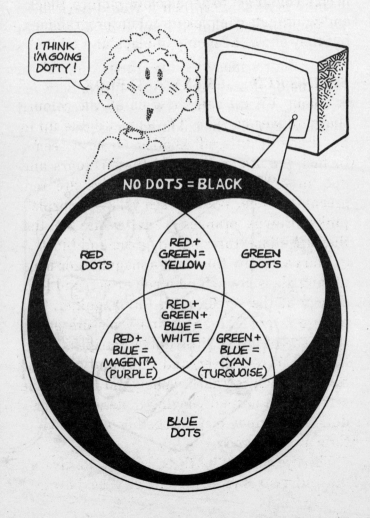

THREE IN ONE

It's a very good thing that our eyes can mix just three colours to form a full-colour picture. It means that colour television need only send three colours. If colour television had to send hundreds of shades, then it would have to be so complicated that it probably would not work!

A colour camera is like three cameras in one. Inside it are three picture tubes. Between the lens and the tubes are pieces of coloured glass. They split the coloured image formed by

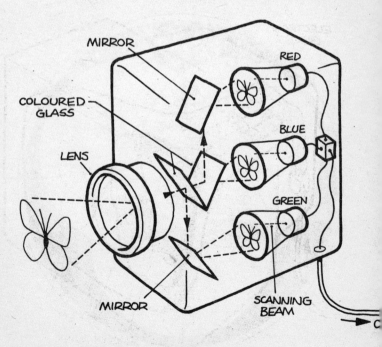

the lens into a red image, a green image and a blue image. It's just like looking at a scene through a piece of coloured glass or plastic. The red, green and blue images form on the three picture tubes. Each tube scans its image, just as in a black-and-white camera. It changes the image brightness into an electric signal.

Three electric signals come from the three tubes. The strengths of the signals depend on the colour in each part of the picture. For example, a bright yellow part gives strong red and green signals, but a weak blue signal. The

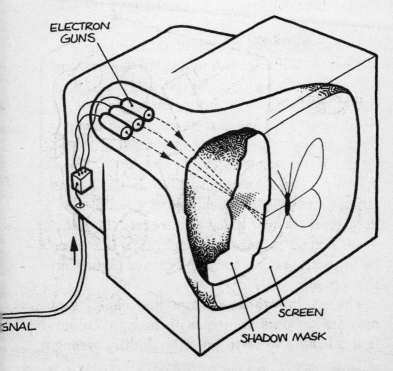

ELECTRON GUNS

SIGNAL

SCREEN

SHADOW MASK

camera then mixes the three signals together to give one colour signal. The station sends out this signal from its masts, or a satellite, or along a cable. It may record the colour signal on a video recorder first and send out the colour programme later.

GETTING YOUR COLOUR BACK

A colour TV set gets the colour signal from its aerial or cable. It then changes the colour signal back into the red signal, green signal and blue signal that come from the camera. These three signals go to the picture tube in the set.

The picture tube is like the picture tube in a black-and-white set. But instead of one electron gun, it has three guns. The red, green and blue signals go to the three guns. Each one fires an electron beam at the screen. On the screen are the dots or stripes, which are made of three kinds of materials called phosphors. These light up in red, green and blue as the beams strike them. The 'red' beam gives a red picture, the 'green' beam a green picture and the 'blue' beam a blue picture. Our eyes mix the three pictures so that we see a full-colour picture on the screen.

The set has to make sure that each beam only strikes dots or stripes of the right colour. If the beams were to go only slightly wrong, then the colours would look very strange! So the picture tube contains a device that sends the three beams to exactly the right phosphors. This is nothing more than a thin sheet full of tiny holes. It's called a shadow mask.

The shadow mask lies just behind the screen. As the three electron beams scan across the screen, they pass through the holes in the shadow mask. In front of each hole is a group of three dots or stripes in red, green and blue. The three electron guns are placed so that when each beam passes through any hole, it always strikes a dot or stripe of the right colour. As you could see through the magnifier, each group of dots or stripes lights up to make each part of the picture the right colour.

MODEL MASK

You can make a model of the shadow mask and screen to show how it works. Make three small holes in a sheet of cardboard as shown on page 72. You can use a pencil to do this, but take care. Then mark three groups of red, green and blue circles on a piece of paper as shown. These are the groups of dots or stripes on the screen. Fix the paper in front of the cardboard, which is the shadow mask. Switch on a torch; this is an electron gun and the light beam is the electron beam.

Hold the torch behind the centre of the

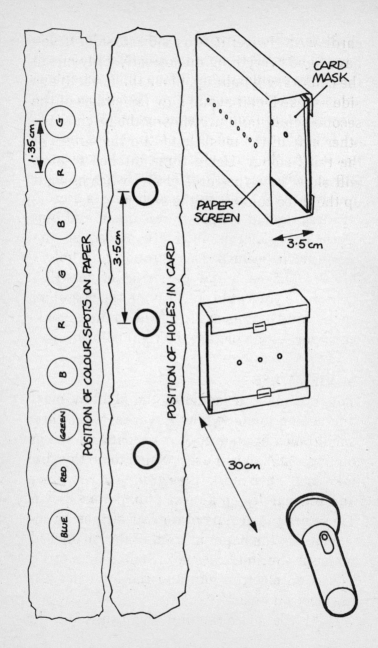

POSITION OF COLOUR SPOTS ON PAPER

G
R
B
G
R
B
GREEN
RED
BLUE

1·35 cm

POSITION OF HOLES IN CARD

3·5 cm

CARD MASK

PAPER SCREEN

3·5 cm

30 cm

cardboard. Swivel it from side to side. If you have lined everything up correctly, only one of the colours will light up. Move the torch to one side and swivel it again; now the circles of the second colour light up. Moving the torch to the other side of the mask lights up the circles of the third colour. Using three torches at once will show how the three electron beams light up the three colours on the screen.

CHAPTER **10**

TV TRICKS

OH LOOK, THE PICTURE HAS GONE INTO SLOW MOTION!

*T*elevision can show us a magical world — as if a witch or wizard had cast a spell on everything. On television, time can suddenly slip back so that an action happens again. Then it often happens slowly, as if time were crawling by in a dream. Then a scene may suddenly shrink in size and start spinning round. Or we may even see people suddenly appearing in all kinds of places, perhaps even flying over mountains!

What we are seeing is not real, nor is it magic. All these strange events are tricks called special effects. They make special use of the way in which television works.

ACTION AND REACTION

A goal in a football match or a terrific stroke in a game of tennis is very exciting. But it may happen so fast that we can miss some of the action. With television, we see an exciting moment again right away. It's called action replay.

As well as sending out pictures of the action in a sport, the TV cameras also send the pictures to a special video recorder. The recorder stores the pictures on tape. To see an action again, the recorder quickly winds the tape back and plays the pictures again. During the replay, we see the picture from the video recorder instead of the cameras. The tape can play back slowly to slow down the action. It may even stop to show a still picture.

You can use a home video recorder to see how action replay works. You can record a match, then rewind to replay just the exciting moments. Pause the recorder to freeze an action. The recorder may have a slow motion button to play the tape slowly.

LETTERS AND NUMBERS

Television also uses computers for special effects. On the picture, we often see a caption —like someone's name in big letters. The name is first typed into a computer at the television studio. When the name is needed, the computer sends out the letters in the form of an electric signal. This caption signal mixes with the picture signal from the cameras. Up comes the name on the screen.

Computers can also spin pictures and produce many other unusual effects. First, the picture signal from the camera is fed into the computer. The computer changes the brightness and colour of all the tiny parts of the picture into code numbers. It stores the numbers in its memory. The computer then alters the order of the numbers, before changing them back into a picture signal. When you see the picture, the tiny parts of it appear in different places on the screen. This changes the picture, so that it appears to spin for example.

You can show how special effects turn a picture back to front. Look at this list of numbers:

```
10111111    11000011
00111110    11000011
00111101    11011011
11000011    11011011
```

It is a set of the brightness numbers that we used in the TV game in Chapter 6. They come from a picture of a dog.

The television computer stores a set of numbers like this. Then it alters them. Do this by

writing down the numbers, but start each row
at the other end like this:

11111101	11000011
01111100	11000011
10111100	11011011
11000011	11011011

Now send these numbers to make a picture as
explained on page 50. Fill in the squares to
form the picture. You have turned the dog back
to front!

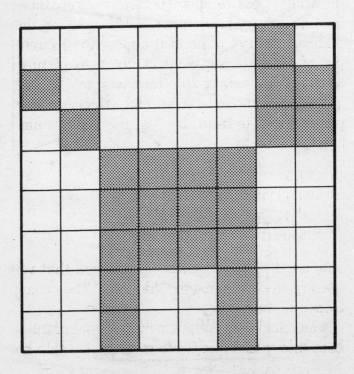

FLYING HIGH

If you appeared on television, one amazing effect could make you fly, even though you would never actually leave the ground. This special effect is called chromakey. It puts two separate pictures together. One is a picture of you in the studio. The other is a picture taken high in the air from an aircraft. Putting the two together makes you appear to fly through the air.

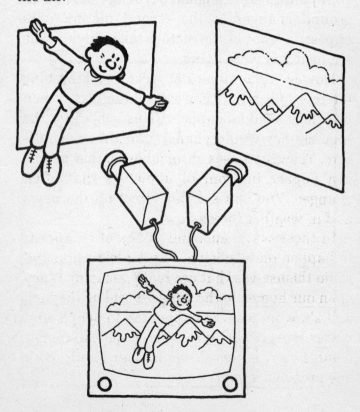

In the studio, you would stand in front of a coloured background and pretend to fly. The colour has to be one of the three colours used in television, and it is usually blue. One camera takes your picture. Another camera uses a film taken from an aircraft. Then a special machine puts the two pictures together. It takes away blue from your picture and puts the second picture in its place. But the other colours in your picture are not changed. So the blue background changes to the second picture. You appear in front of the picture taken high in the air, as if you were flying.

However, you must not wear anything blue for this to work. If you wore blue jeans, then your legs would disappear! This is because the blue clothes would change into the other picture. Television uses chromakey so that people can appear in front of a picture that often changes. You can see this effect on the news and in weather forecasts.

In these ways, amazing things often appear to happen on television. But it's television and radio themselves that are really amazing. They open our homes to the whole world as they tell and show us what is happening to people and places everywhere. We can now see and understand how we are all one human family with one precious home.

INDEX